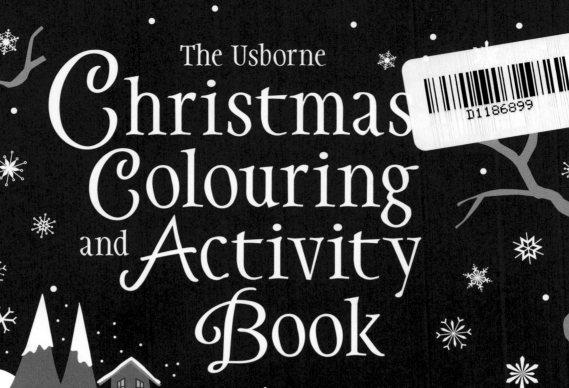

The Usborne
Christmas
Colouring
and Activity
Book

Designed and illustrated
by Candice Whatmore

Additional illustration by Lizzie Barber

Written by Kirsteen Rogers

About this book

On each right-hand page there is a black and white picture for you
to colour. Fill in the white spaces in any way you like. (For hints and tips on
colouring, go to page 32.) The left-hand pages are full of suggestions for
doodling and creating pictures of your own. If you'd like to cut out
your finished pictures, just cut along the dotted lines.

Doodle snowmen

Draw heads, arms and
clothes on the snowmen.
Give them eyes and
carroty noses.

Decorate the tree

Draw over the dotted lines
to make a Christmas tree
and presents of your own,
then decorate them.

Write a letter to Santa

At the North Pole, Santa's elves are working hard, making and wrapping up presents.

Write a letter to Santa and draw pictures of the presents you'd like him to bring you.

Write your address here.

Dear Santa,

I have been very good. Here are some presents I would love to find in my stocking:

Thank you. I hope you are well.

From ....

Sign your name here.

Draw some penguins

The penguins are having great fun
gliding and sliding across the ice.

Draw wings and feet on these
penguin bodies.

Use this body shape to
design your own penguin.

Fill the jars with goodies

The sweetshop window is full of chocolates, fudge, lollipops and sugar canes.

Fill the jars with sweets.

Add more jars of your own.

Draw some chocolate boxes.

sweetie shop

Christmas presents

Design your own Christmas giftwrap patterns on the presents below.

Draw dangly decorations

Decorate the twisty branches with baubles, stars and bells.

Fairy dresses

Finish and decorate these
dresses, and design a fairy
crown to match each one.

Midnight town

Draw chimneys, windows and doors on the houses below.

Then draw over the dotted lines to make some houses of your own. Add tiles, bricks and other details.

Colour the stockings

Draw over the dotted lines and then decorate the stockings any way you like.

A snack for Santa

Draw over the dotted lines to make a plate,
then fill it with things for Santa to eat.

To Santa
love from

Add your name here.

Menu ideas

Mince pies
Fairy cakes
Chocolate log
A slice of Christmas cake
A mug of cocoa
A glass of milk
(or something stronger)
A bunch of carrots
(for the reindeer)

Christmas angels

Draw instruments for these angels to play. One of them has a harp, one has a trumpet and one has tinkling bells.

Fill the sky with snowflakes

Use the guides on this page to make
up your own snowflake designs.

Ice the cakes

Decorate these cakes and biscuits by drawing icing swirls, sugar sprinkles and sweets.

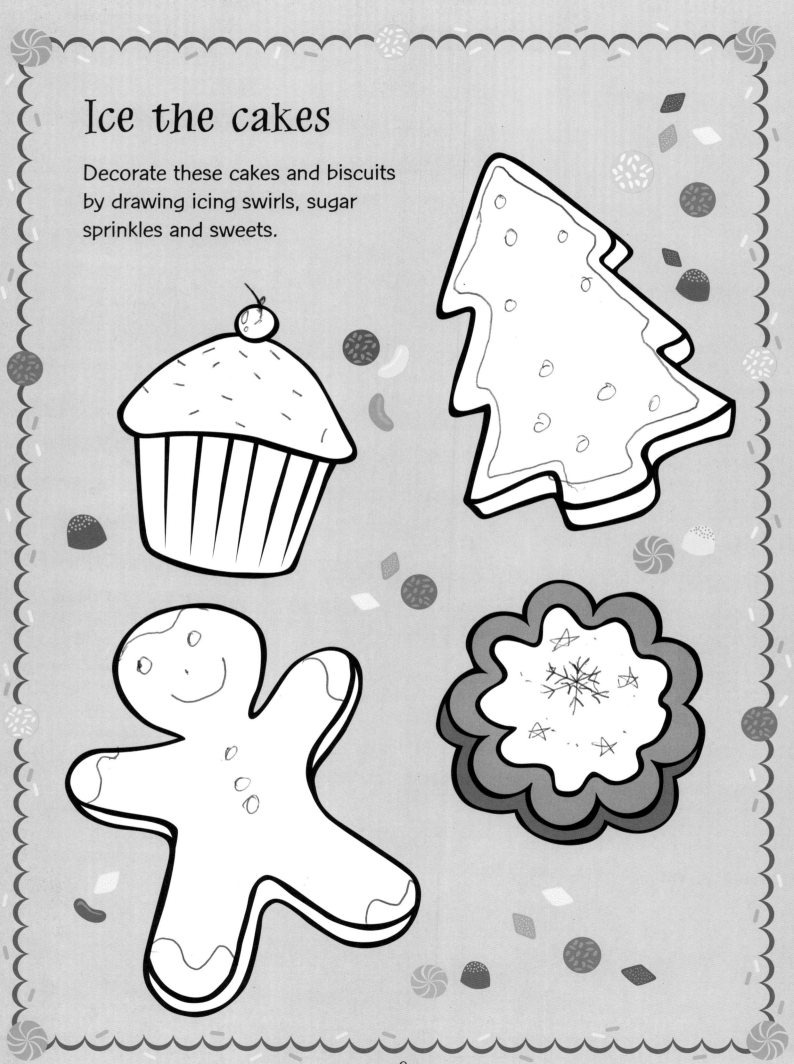

Create a firework display

Whoosh! Bang! Wheeeeee!
It's New Year's Eve and
the night sky is ablaze
with fizzing fireworks.

Fill this page with sizzling firework explosions.

Add trails of sparkling stars to these rockets.

Colouring hints and tips

Use felt-tip pens or coloured pencils to colour in the pictures. Felt-tip pens will give you strong colours, while pencils will have a softer effect.

You can draw patterns within some of the shapes. For example, these presents are filled with...

...spots and dots...

...stars...

...zigzags and stripes.

Fill in shapes with only one colour, like this star trail behind the sleigh...

...or use lots of different pens.

You could finish this picture to practise colouring.

Fill in large areas, such as Santa's sleigh, with lots of lines going in the same direction.

It's a good idea to lay your book on a flat surface while you are colouring, or slip a piece of cardboard under the page you are filling in, to make a firm surface.

If you want to cut out your picture, you'll find a dotted line on each page to cut along.

This edition first published in 2012 by Usborne Publishing Ltd., 83-85 Saffron Hill, London ECIN 8RT, England.
Copyright © 2012, 2008 Usborne Publishing Ltd. The name Usborne and the devices 🖋️ 🏠 are Trade Marks of Usborne Publishing Ltd.